STEM Projects in **MINECRAFT**®

The Unofficial Guide to
Using Math in
MINECRAFT®

JILL KEPPELER

PowerKiDS press.

New York

Published in 2020 by The Rosen Publishing Group, Inc.
29 East 21st Street, New York, NY 10010

First Edition

Editor: Greg Roza
Book Design: Rachel Rising
Illustrator: Matías Lapegüe

Photo Credits: Cover, pp. 1, 3, 4, 6, 8, 10, 12, 14, 16, 18, 20, 22, 23, 24 (background) Evgeniy Dzyuba/Shutterstock.com; pp. 6, 8, 10, 12, 18 (inset) Levent Konuk/Shutterstock.com; p. 7 Panksvatouny/Shutterstock.com; p.15 Glen Wiltshire/Shutterstock.com; p. 17 Claudia Norberg Schulz/Shutterstock.com; p. 22 pikselstock/Shutterstock.com.

Cataloging-in-Publication Data

Names: Keppeler, Jill.
Title: The unofficial guide to using math in Minecraft ® / Jill Keppeler.
Description: New York : PowerKids Press, 2020. | Series: STEM projects in Minecraft | Includes glossary and index.
Identifiers: ISBN 9781725310667 (pbk.) | ISBN 9781725310681 (library bound) | ISBN 9781725310674 (6 pack)
Subjects: LCSH: Mathematics–Juvenile literature. | Minecraft (Game) – Juvenile literature.
Classification: LCC GV1469.M55 K47 2020 | DDC 794.8–dc23

Manufactured in the United States of America

CPSIA Compliance Information: Batch #CWPK20. For Further Information contact Rosen Publishing, New York, New York at 1-800-237-9932.

Contents

Math and *Minecraft?*

There are many cool things about the game of *Minecraft.* You can explore a huge world and find new things. You can fight monsters. You can build amazing structures and decorate them however you please.

But do you know that *Minecraft* can help you learn math? Maybe that doesn't sound like a lot of fun, but math skills can help you survive and create in your game world. Math can show you how to fight and travel **efficiently** and how to make and acquire new items and tools to help you survive. Math and geometry are very useful in *Minecraft!*

Geometry is the form of math that deals with points, lines, angles, shapes, surfaces, and solids. The basic **unit** of geometry in *Minecraft* is the cube.

Smelt This

Heating items in a furnace is a common way to produce **resources** in *Minecraft*. Many blocks can be heated to produce other items. You can **smelt** gold or iron ores to make gold or iron **ingots**. You can cook fish, meat, or potatoes. You can melt sand into glass.

However, you need fuel to do this. Many *Minecraft* items can be used as fuel. You can use math to figure out how much fuel you need. A piece of coal or charcoal will heat eight items. So, how much coal would you need to heat a full stack (64) of pieces of something?

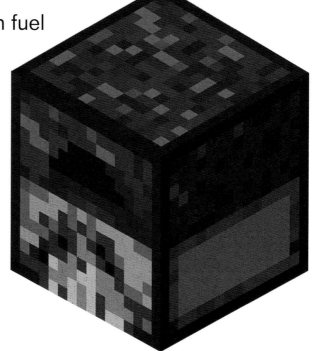

MINECRAFT MANIA

You can experiment to find out how much of various types of fuels you need to heat things. A block of wood will heat 1.5 items. A bucket of lava will heat 100 items!

This worker is smelting steel. You can't make steel in *Minecraft*, but you can smelt iron.

GOLD ORE

GOLD INGOT

COAL

Building Blocks

You can use math to help you figure out how many resources you need to make a building in *Minecraft.* To figure out how big your building should be, figure out what you want to put inside it.

For example, say you want a bed, a crafting table, a furnace, and a double chest in your first house. A bed and a double chest take up two blocks each. A crafting table and a furnace take up one block each. You'll want some room to walk around. How much space do you think you need inside your house?

MINECRAFT MANIA

You can dig out a cave instead of building a structure for your first base if you want. You'll need fewer resources, but you'll still need to figure out how much space you'll want.

It can help to draw a plan of what you want to build. You can draw what your house will look like outside, but you can also draw an inside view to help you plan how big it should be.

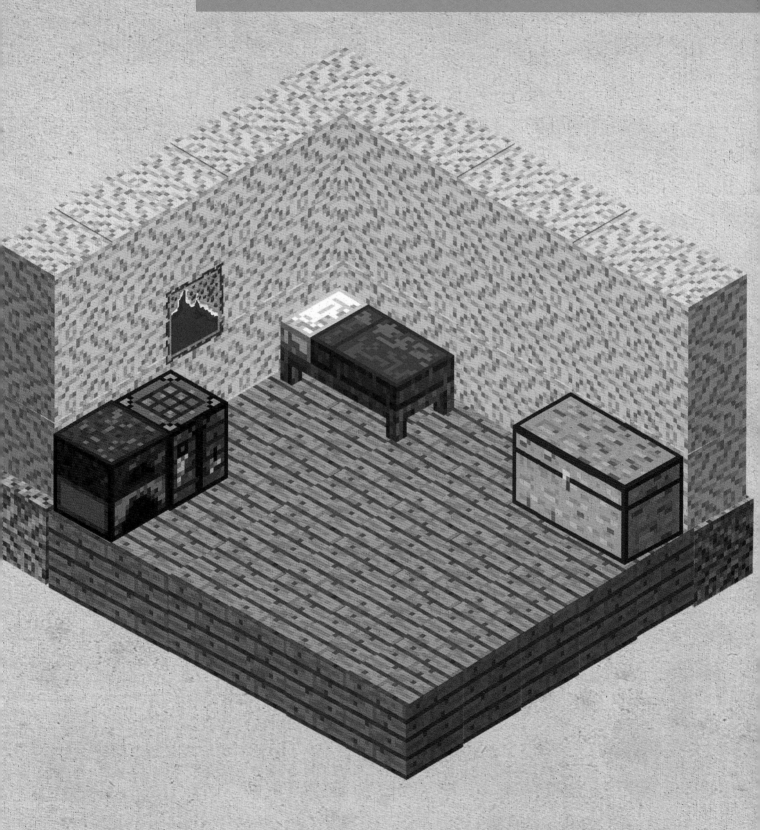

Book Smart

If you're playing in Survival **mode** in *Minecraft*, you need to collect all the resources you'll use. That means it can be important to plan out what you need and how to get it. For example, you need three pieces of sugar cane to make three pieces of paper.

To make a book, you need three pieces of paper and a piece of leather. To make a bookshelf, you need three books and some wood. To get an enchanting table to work at top level, you need 15 bookshelves. How much sugar cane will you need for that?

MINECRAFT MANIA

An enchanting table will put an enchantment, or magic spell, on many *Minecraft* items, including armor, weapons, and tools.

You'll need a book, four blocks of obsidian, and two diamonds to make an enchanting table. Different arrangements of bookshelves around an enchanting table will get you different results.

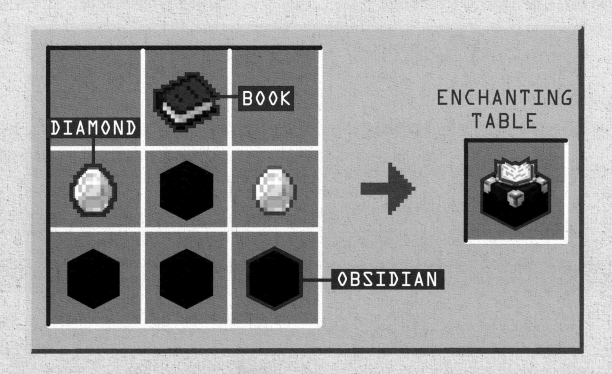

DIAMOND

BOOK

ENCHANTING TABLE

OBSIDIAN

How Many Hits?

Say you've been exploring your *Minecraft* world and you get caught outside after dark. There's a zombie coming at you and you swing your sword. How many times will you have to hit it to kill it? That depends on what kind of weapon you have.

A zombie has 20 health points. If you have a wooden sword, it will do 4 or 5 points of **damage** every time you hit the zombie. How many hits will it take? If you have a diamond sword, it will do 7 or 8 points of damage each time. How many hits will that take?

MINECRAFT MANIA

Mobs in *Minecraft* each have their own amount of health points. Creepers and skeletons also have 20 points. Endermen have 40 points. Iron golems have 100! Chickens have only 4 health points.

Humans have used swords a long time. We've made swords from copper, bronze, iron, or steel. In *Minecraft*, you can make swords from wood, stone, gold, iron, or diamond.

CHICKEN

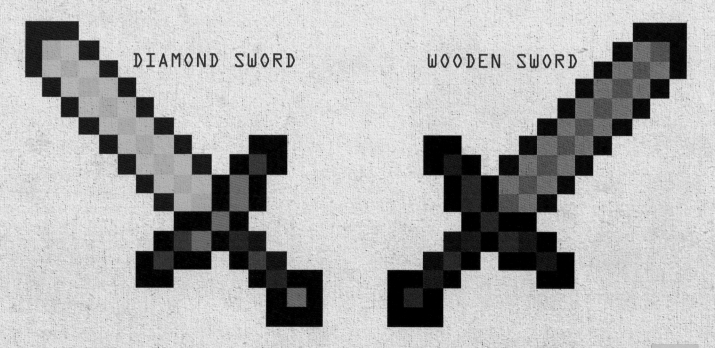

DIAMOND SWORD

WOODEN SWORD

Enchanting

If you have an enchantment on your sword, your math might be a little different. The Sharpness enchantment means you'll do 1 to 6 more points of damage with each swing of your sword, depending on the level of the enchantment and the **version** of the game. Other enchantments can affect the damage, too.

Other weapons in *Minecraft* do different amounts of damage. This includes bows and arrows, axes, tridents, and crossbows. Each of those can hold enchantments (such as Power for bows and **Impaling** for tridents) as well. Experiment and do the math to see how much damage they can cause.

MINECRAFT MANIA

With bows and crossbows, the amount of damage is also affected by how far you've charged, or drawn, them. A bow with no charge does 1 point of damage. A fully charged bow can do 10 points of damage.

TRIDENT

BOW

POTION

If you drink a **potion** of Strength, your attacks will also do more damage—up to 6 extra points with each attack!

Village Traders

If you find a village in *Minecraft,* you can trade with the villagers to get useful items. But when is it worth it to trade? You can use math to figure that out.

For example, say you have a stack of 64 pieces of string collected. A fisherman villager may buy 16 pieces of string for an emerald. However, you can also turn your string into blocks of white wool. A shepherd villager will buy 16 blocks of white wool for an emerald. What should you do? Does it help if you know it takes four pieces of string to make a block of wool?

Say a farmer villager will trade you an emerald for 20 pieces of wheat. You want 12 emeralds so you can buy a diamond axe from another villager. How much wheat do you need?

17

Nether Travel

You can only reach *Minecraft's* Nether **dimension** through an obsidian **portal**. The dimension is full of lava and deadly mobs. However, you can use the Nether to travel more quickly through the game's Overworld.

A block in the Nether is equal to eight blocks in the Overworld. To travel 8,000 blocks in the Overworld, you'd have to travel 1,000 blocks in the Nether. You can create a Nether portal in or near your base, travel through the Nether, and then built another portal and go back to the Overworld. Be sure you're at least 128 Nether blocks away, though, or you'll come out the same portal.

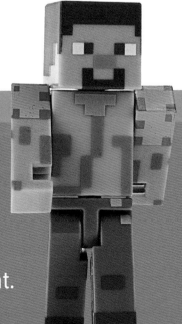

MINECRAFT MANIA

Once you've built your Nether portal frame, you'll need to light it to create the purple portal. You can use flint and steel, a tool made with one iron ingot and a piece of flint.

You need at least 10 blocks of obsidian to build a Nether portal frame. Portals should be at least five blocks high and four blocks wide, but you can take out the corners to use less obsidian.

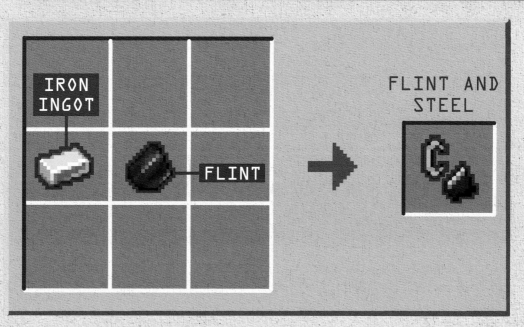

IRON INGOT

FLINT

FLINT AND STEEL

Redstone

Redstone and redstone dust can act like electricity in *Minecraft*. It's possible to build amazing things with them and other tools. You'll need math and geometry to figure out how best to build redstone machines.

A redstone power source, such as a redstone block or redstone torch, can only send power for 15 blocks. Redstone wire, created by putting redstone dust on a surface, carries power. The power level drops with every block the wire crosses. A redstone repeater will strengthen the power level. To send power 40 blocks away from your power source, how many redstone repeaters will you need?

<-- redstone block

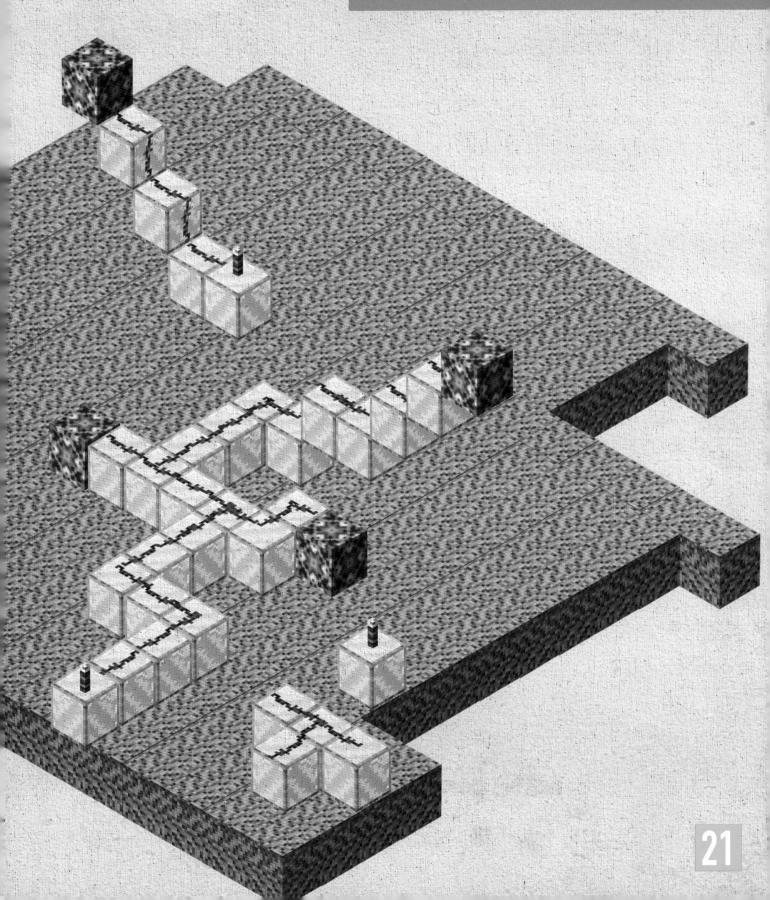

A redstone **circuit** might include a power source, wires, switches, lights, and more. *Minecraft* players have built huge machines powered by redstone. What can you build?

Making Mods

You can make your *Minecraft* creations even more exciting with modifications, or mods. Using a computer program called ScriptCraft, you can create new blocks, change the way the game functions, and make your own games. Imagine what you could create! You could create blocks that are bigger or smaller than usual, or you could create weapons that do even more damage. What about creating new kinds of villagers?

If you're interested in learning how to create mods in *Minecraft*, visit the website below. You'll find the information needed to get started with ScriptCraft and build your own *Minecraft* mods.

https://scriptcraftjs.org/

Glossary

circuit: A closed path of wires through which electricity can travel.

damage: Loss or harm done to a person or piece of property.

dimension: A level of existence or a world.

efficiently: Done in the quickest, best way possible.

impale: To send a pointed object into or through.

ingot: Metal made into a shape for storage or transportation.

mob: A moving creature within *Minecraft*. Often used to mean one of the monsters that spawns, or appears, in *Minecraft* at night.

mode: A form of something that is different from other forms of the same thing.

portal: A large door or gate to someplace else.

potion: A drink meant to have a special effect on someone.

resource: Something that can be used.

smelt: To heat to separate metals.

unit: A particular amount of something that's used as a standard for counting, measuring, or building.

version: A form of something that is different from the ones that came before it.

Index

Websites

Due to the changing nature of Internet links, PowerKids Press has developed
an online list of websites related to the subject of this book. This site is
updated regularly. Please use this link to access the list:
www.powerkidslinks.com/stemmc/math